How to Become a Unicorn

ISBN: 9798586677051

Los Angeles, CA

First Paperback Edition

To Tenn
Keep Glowing

How To Become a Unicorn

Illustrated and written
By Ingrid De La O

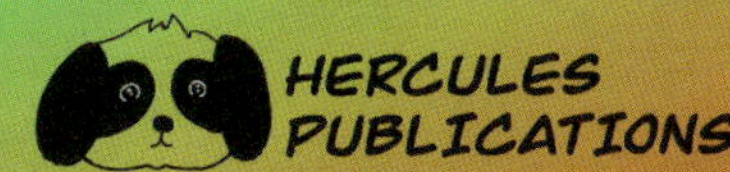

I AM BLACK AND WHITE
I WANT TO BE BRIGHT
I WANT TO TAKE A FLIGHT

My colors are boring
Not much exploring

Unicorns are beautiful
They are colorful
Joyful
Some are purple

How do I become a unicorn?
I wear a uniform
Should I transform into a unicorn?

I might need a
few things

I might need a
set of "wings!"

UNICORN
PAINT

A touch of glistening white
An inch of starlight
Before this night,
I might take a flight!

UNICORN
GLOW PAINT
UNICORN
PAINT

WHAT SHOULD I DO FOR A HORN?
HOW ABOUT A CORN?!

A MAGIC GLOW!
A RAINBOW SHOW!
OFF TO THE MEADOWS I GO!

I SMELL THE FLOWERS
I SEE THE COLORS
I'M LIKE NO OTHER!

I see the sparkles
The twinkles and the dazzles!

It only took a thunder
To make me plunder

My paint dripped
My wings ripped
My corn chipped

How am I still glowing?
My heart is overflowing

My reflection is imperfection
And that is perfection

It turns out
My heart glows throughout

I don't need to pretend
To be able to blend

I AM

ENOUGH!

Ingrid De La O wrote and illustrated this book. She also wrote this bio in the third person because it sounds much cooler when someone writes about you.

She's currently existing in Los Angeles and writes children's books with the direction of her 6-year-old son Tenn.

Her previous hits include "Perry's Waste of Time" and "Zeusy The Blue Troll," sold in your favorite online store, which is Amazon (am I wrong?).

Find her on Instagram: @ingriddelao.

Or send her an email at ingriddelao@gmail.com for inquiries, relationship advice, smoothie recipes, weather reports, or whatever you need criticism for. She's there for you.

Printed in Great Britain
by Amazon

69565598R00024